DK READERS

BEGINNING 1 TO READ

Little Dolphin

Written by Sue Unstead

Little Dolphin lives
in the sparkly blue sea.
As soon as he was born,
his mama took him
up, up, up to snatch
his very first breath
of air.

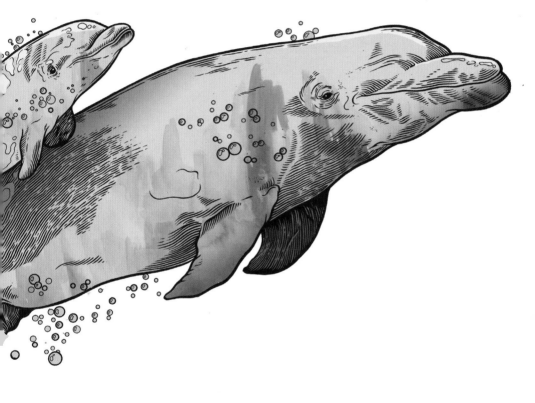

Mama calls to Little Dolphin
all the time.
"Wheee, wheee!
Where are you?"

Little Dolphin calls back to her.
He has his own song,
"Wheee, whooooa!
Here I am, Mama."

Little Dolphin stays close
to his mama.
She teaches him how to dive
and how to leap over
the waves.
But he longs to play with
the bigger dolphins.

"When can I join them?"
he asks.
"When you can swim fast,
Little Dolphin," says Mama.

Little Dolphin grows bigger
every day.
"I can swim fast.
I can leap and dive," he says.
Mama says, "Now you are
ready for Dolphin School.
Remember to stay
with the other dolphins.
Watch the leader.
Look out for big boats."

Little Dolphin swims away
with a swish of his tail.
He joins the other dolphins.
They play follow-the-leader.
They play catch-that-fish.
They see who can jump
the highest.
"Wheee, wheeoa."
"Click-click-click."

13

Rrrr, rumble, rumble, rrrr.

"Listen! What is that sound?" asks the biggest dolphin.

"A ship! It is a ship's engine,"
cries another dolphin.
"Quick! Let's chase it,"
says the biggest dolphin.

Here comes the ship!
A foamy wave pushes through
the water.
"Wheee!
Let's dive under it.
Whooah!
Let's jump in front of it,"
say the dolphins.

Splash! Splash!

"This is fun!" says Little Dolphin.

There is a dark shadow
above them.
Little Dolphin hears the thump
of the engine.
He feels the swoosh
from the propellers.
"Oooh! It is scary,"
thinks Little Dolphin.
He swims fast.

19

"Help! I cannot keep up,"
says Little Dolphin.
"The ship is too fast for me.
Where is everyone?
Click-click-click."

No one answers.

Little Dolphin is alone.

"Wheee, whoa, Maaama!"

he cries.

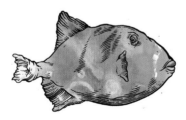

Whoosh!

Little Dolphin pops his head
out of the water.
"Look! There is a white sail.
It must be a boat.
I will follow you,"
thinks Little Dolphin.
A girl on board the boat
sees Little Dolphin.
The girl is called Rosie.

23

The fishing boat chugs back
to port.
Little Dolphin follows,
tired and lost.
"You must go back out
to sea," says Rosie.
She runs to fetch
her own small boat.
"I must save Little Dolphin,"
she thinks.

She remembers what her own
mama told her when she was
a young girl.
"Stay with the school,
watch the leader, and
look out for big boats,"
she thinks.

"Follow me, Little Dolphin,"
she calls.
Little Dolphin follows
her small boat.

Out in the bay, Little Dolphin
hears his mama calling,
"Wheee, whee!
Where are you?"
"Wheee, whooa!" he cries.
"Here I am, Mama!"

Rosie sees two dolphins leaping.
She thinks they are smiling, too.
What a happy day!

Dolphin Facts

Smart dolphins

Dolphins are clever animals and love to play.

Friendly dolphins

They live in groups of 10 to 12 dolphins called pods, or schools.

Long life

A dolphin can live for 25 years.

Hold your breath

A dolphin usually comes up to the surface for breath every two minutes, but can hold its breath for much longer.

Index

DK READERS help children learn to read, then read to learn. If you enjoyed this DK READER, then look out for these other titles for your child.

Level 1 Deadly Dinosaurs
Roar! Thud! Meet Rexy, Sid, Deano, and Sonia, the dinosaurs that come alive at night in the museum. Who do you think is the deadliest?

Level 1 Playful Puppy
Holly's dream has come true—she's been given her very own puppy. Share her delight in the playfulness of her new puppy as she tries to train him.

Level 1 Bugs Hide and Seek
Surprise! Some bugs have the perfect shape and color to stay hidden. They look like the plants around them. Can you spot them?

Level 1 Mega Machines
Hard hats on! The mega machines are very busy building a new school. Watch them in action!

Level 1 Pirate Attack!
Come and join Captain Blackbeard and his pirate crew for an action-packed adventure on the high seas.